CARS

FORD TRUCK

Michael Bradley

mc **Marshall Cavendish**
Benchmark
New York

Marshall Cavendish Benchmark
99 White Plains Road
Tarrytown, NY 10591-5502
www.marshallcavendish.us

All Internet sites were available and accurate when sent to press.

Library of Congress Cataloging-in-Publication Data

Bradley, Michael.
Ford truck / by Michael Bradley.
p. cm. — (Cars)
ISBN 978-0-7614-2979-1
1. Ford trucks—Parts—Catalogs. I. Title.
TL230.5.F57B73 2008
629.223'2—dc22
2007029489

Photo research by Connie Gardner

Cover photo by © Ron Kimball Stock Photography/Ron Kimball

The photographs in this book are used by permission and through the courtesy of: *Getty Images*: Time and Life
Pictures, back cover; AP Photo: David Zalubowski, 3; Ford, 14 (B); *The Image Works*: © National Motor Museum/
Topham-HIP, 4; Jim Sully/Newscast, 21; *Ford Communication Services/Ford Still Image Library*: 5, 22, 23, 24 (T & B);
From the Collections of The Henry Ford: 6 (T); 12, 15, 16; *RonKimball/www.kimballstock.com*: 6 (B), 9, 13, 25, 27, 29.

Publisher: Michelle Bisson
Art Director: Anahid Hamparian
Series Designer: Daniel Roode

Printed in Malaysia
1 3 5 6 4 2

CONTENTS

SERIES F-6

MAX. GROSS VEHICLE WEIGHT: 15,500 lbs.
NOMINAL TONNAGE RATING: 2 Tons
WHEELBASES: 134-inch and 158-inch
MODELS AVAILABLE: 9 and 12 ft. platform and stake bodies; Chassis with cab; with windshield; with cowl.

BIG, BIG, EXTRA BIG CHASSIS FOR

DOUBLE C
built-in ch
ments ext
rear sprin
frame thr
span, pro
two plane

QUADRAX 2-SPEED AXLE has two performance ranges. Single reduction high speed range saves gas, oil, engine maintenance. Double reduction low speed range offers more pulling ability.

REMOVABLE BRAKE DRUMS simplify maintenance. Drums can be bought separately from hubs for replacement.

BRIDGE-TYPE BO
form and stake
gage steel. Si
steel cross mem
stand up under

NEW ROUGE 239 TRUCK V-8 Completely new! New cylinder block! New cylinder heads! New valves! New crankshaft! New camshaft! New oil-saver features! New gas-saver features! Top power for big time trucking!

In 1947 Ford introduced the F-Series trucks. The F-6 advertised in this poster was one of the biggest pickups on the market.

ENGINEERING HIGHLIGHTS—NEW FORD F-6

NEW ROUGE 239 TRUCK V-8—New engine-top setting of engine accessories—Replaceable-type main and individual connecting rod bearings—Alloy intake and exhaust valve seat inserts for longer wear—New, Series-Flow cooling for better temperature control, prevents hot spots—New horizontal plane intake manifold, more uniform fuel charge, all cylinders—New Loadomatic spark control for more power, more economy. New Rouge 226 Truck Six available. **CHASSIS**—Feather-Foot hydraulic brakes, fixed anchor type, plus vacuum actuation for true and easy stopping—Roll-action needle bearing steering control—Gyro-Grip clutch multiplies grip with increased speed—4-speed transmission with separate clutch housing for easier servicing—Double channel frame provides high stiffness in *two* planes.

NEW MILLION DOLLAR CAB features new 3-way air control, new coach-type seat for comfort. New Level Action mounting to frame for longer cab life. New Spiralounge seat with variable-rate spiral coil spring and hydraulic shock absorber available for comfort-plus.

POWER BRAKING—Vacuum actuation relieves muscle power needed at the brake pedal, multiplies the foot pressure over 100%, retains normal "brake feel" for responsive, easy braking.

platheavyed to uilt to ment.

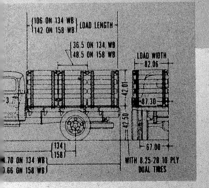

CHAPTER ONE
A BIG CHANCE

One million dollars a day. That's how much Ford Motor Company was losing in 1947. And the company was on the verge of closing down. Chevrolet had control of the country's truck buyers, and Ford needed something big to change the **momentum**. The company was still selling plenty of cars and trucks, but it had lost its lead. Ford was America's first motor company, but in 1947, it wasn't the most popular anymore. So, what do you do when you need to make money? Spend it, of course.

This 1948 model sports a new windshield design and the roomy "Million Dollar Cab."

That's what Ford did. It invested $30 million in its new F-Series trucks. And it was money well spent. Chevy may have had a new line of trucks, but Ford was about to answer with a bang. The F-Series came with a six or **eight-cylinder engine**. Its wider, higher "Million Dollar Cab" had a radio and a **spiralounge seat** that was more comfortable than the seats in any other truck. It had a new grill with built-in headlights and a one-piece windshield. Ford called it "Star-Spangled New" and let everybody know that its new product was "Modern!" and "Strikingly Different!" You know what? It was just that.

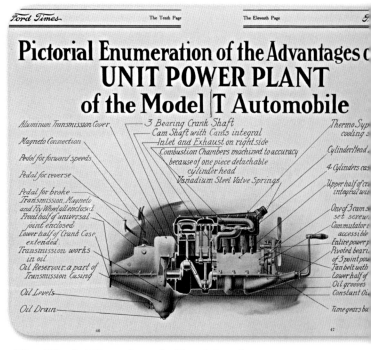

The Model T and early Ford trucks ran on four-cylinder engines. To start the engine, drivers would manually turn the handle on the right.

Ford developed the first pickup truck in 1925. This 1934 Ford was designed to work as a tow truck.

The 1964 Ford F-100 was available in only a handful of colors, including Caribbean Turquoise. The owner even has a matching Serro Scotty trailer!

By 1956 Ford had sold 420,000 of its F-100 trucks, its best performance ever. A decade earlier the company had been struggling, but now it was flying high. The tool Henry Ford had developed to make life easier for the farmer had come to the rescue. A new American symbol of toughness had been born.

Though it began operations in 1903, Ford didn't start making trucks until twenty-one years later. Since then, it has had a hand in just about every possible area of American—and international— business with its trucks. Ford has made vans, buses, tractor-trailers, heavy-duty **haulers**, and anything else built for hard work.

Its most popular product, of course, has been the pickup. It is designed for a variety of uses and serves families, businesspeople, farmers, and anybody else who needs a vehicle with some extra power and cargo room.

Even though it took the introduction of the F-Series to help Ford move out of its slump, there is no denying the company's position at the **forefront** of truck production in America. From the moment it introduced its first factory-built truck in 1925, Ford was a leader. It developed the first pickup truck. It was able to keep moving forward during the **Great Depression**, when money was tight and sales dropped. Still, Ford boasted a line of thirty-eight cars and trucks.

Today, Ford offers its signature F-Series, with plenty of variety. There are "Supercabs" for those who want more room. There are compact trucks for those with a smaller **budget**. And anybody looking for a vehicle capable of heavy-duty work can find a variety of trucks ready to do the job. That's Ford today. Really, it's what Ford has always been, from the time Henry Ford cranked out the first car in 1903. The Ford truck is a symbol of Americans' desire to work hard.

Ford's F-Series has come a long way since 1947! People still love the size and power of today's Ford trucks, such as this 2007 F-150 King Ranch Lariat.

Ford assembly line workers did many things manually in 1947. Here, the men are fitting the wheels of a truck to the chassis.

Henry Ford's father came to the United States from Ireland, chased across the Atlantic Ocean by a potato **famine** so **severe** that tens of thousands of Irish people starved to death. He was a farmer, and young Henry spent much of his life finding ways to make life easier for those who worked the soil.

His cars and trucks were made to work. They weren't necessarily fast or fancy. They were for people who had a job to do. In 1906 Ford began experimenting with motorized tractors, but he didn't come up with a complete, factory-produced truck until 1925. Before then, if somebody wanted a Ford "truck," they had to buy a Ford Model TT **chassis** and add parts to it from a kit. In 1911 it cost about $350 (a month's wages for many) to purchase the extra parts. By 1917, that cost was up to $600. Even though other companies were offering trucks, most of them also featured the Ford chassis.

By 1925, Ford decided it was time to be in the truck business completely. So, it produced the "Model T Runabout with pickup body." Okay, so it wasn't the catchiest name. But it was a genuine

Before 1925, Ford owners had to add parts to the Model TT if they wanted a truck. It's hard to believe this 1930s chassis, or frame, was once a big pickup truck!

Ford model and cost $281. It featured a closed cab with windows on the doors that could be raised and lowered with cloth straps. For an extra $20 you could get a windshield that opened for better air flow in hot weather. Nearly 34,000 were sold in the first year. It was a huge success, but it didn't eliminate the competition.

Three years later, with Chevrolet taking away some of Ford's sales, Henry Ford designed a new car, the Model A. Americans were so excited by this model that dealers had to call in the mounted police to keep the peace. Ford took more than 500,000 advance orders, including thousands for the Model A truck. It had the same chassis, engine, and **transmission** as the car, but it came in open and closed cabs.

Even though sales dipped considerably during the Great Depression of the 1930s, Ford kept producing cars and trucks. In 1932 it added a V-8 engine to its trucks, a move that would define the Ford line for years to come. During World War II Ford focused on producing vehicles for the military, so the company needed a boost in 1947 from its new F-Series trucks.

In 1953 the F-1 became the F-100, and by 1956, Ford had sold 420,000 F-100 pickups, its biggest total ever. Clearly it was

That's a truck? This 1926 Ford Model T truck is definitely a distant ancestor of the modern version.

The Ford F-100 logo is as distinctive as the truck that bears its trademark.

established as the nation's top truck manufacturer. Ford continued to improve the F-Series line, adding more powerful engines throughout the 1960s, and **debuting** the Ranger, a sport-utility vehicle (SUV), in 1967.

In 1972 Ford introduced a "mini" pickup and two years later put an extended cab truck on the market.

In the 1990s Ford added features to make its pickups look more like models from the late 1950s. This truck has flared fenders around the rear tires. The design was called "the splash."

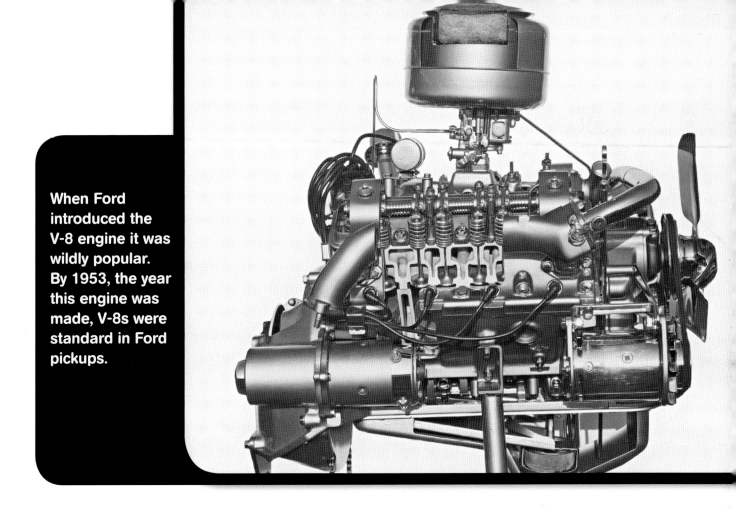

When Ford introduced the V-8 engine it was wildly popular. By 1953, the year this engine was made, V-8s were standard in Ford pickups.

The F-150 debuted in 1975 as a more powerful alternative to the F-100. By 1984 the F-100 had been dropped, leaving the F-150 as Ford's base pickup truck.

The 1990s featured improvements in engine power, cooler designs, and better cab comforts. Ford remained on top of the truck world, but it wasn't about to stop.

There was just too much work left to be done.

In 1936 Ford celebrated the production of its three-millionth truck!

The year was 1936, and America was still fighting its way out from under its greatest economic **crisis**. Ford was struggling, too, trying to keep itself moving forward, despite the tough times.

That didn't mean it wasn't cranking out trucks. In fact, that year Ford produced its three-millionth truck, a DeLuxe Panel Delivery workhorse that had **decals** on it to show it was special. While it went on tour around the country, Ford came up with a promotion to show people just how hard-working its trucks were. It was called the "On-The-Job-Test," and it became very popular.

Anybody who was thinking about buying a Ford truck was invited to dealerships where they could borrow a pickup or heavier-duty model for a couple of days. The idea was that once people saw how the truck could perform under daily **requirements**, they would be sold. Although no official sales figures exist to prove how well the stunt worked, it was successful. And it showed just how valuable the Ford name was to those who worked hard.

That's how Henry Ford saw it when he first started building cars and trucks. He wanted to help the working man. At first, that worker was a farmer, since Ford's father had been a farmer. But as America became more involved in industry and other forms of production, the Ford line adapted. Sure, there was always a push to make the Ford trucks look hipper and more modern. That happened with each new model year. The most important thing, though, was that Ford produced trucks that would work.

During World War II Ford built sea jeeps, which could do anything from cross a river to navigate a lake. The sea jeep even had a built-in pump to bail out water that splashed inside!

So, the company produced tow trucks, buses, tractors, trailers, flatbeds, tankers, and dump trucks. During war time Ford worked for the U.S. Army, producing personnel carriers, four-wheel drive jeep-type vehicles, and other trucks used for hauling and towing ammunition and equipment. The United States had a job to do overseas, and Ford was going to help.

If Ford couldn't produce exactly what its customers wanted, at least it had the **framework**. That's why you'll still see Ford products **outfitted** with tankers, firefighting equipment, and just about anything else needed to keep people working successfully. That's why Ford has always used slogans like "Job Tough" and "Work Force" to describe its trucks. They are designed for people with things to do and serve as excellent partners on the job.

Of course, not all work is done on a construction site or delivery route. Trucks aren't only used to put the fire out or bring the equipment in. Sometimes, driving a truck is about getting the groceries home or the kids to a baseball game, or about taking a family vacation. So, when the SUV boom started, Ford's trucks were a big part of it. The Explorer was first. Then came the bigger, tougher Expedition. A smaller SUV, the Escape, debuted in 2001 with a mission to be as job-friendly as its big brother, but also sporty.

Nobody said being on the job always had to be boring.

In 2004 Ford debuted the Escape Hybrid, which operates on both gas and battery power. It was the first SUV hybrid!

Henry Ford stands with a 1932 Flathead V-8 engine. Drivers loved the affordability and the extra power!

CHAPTER FOUR

THE POWER OF V-8

It was called the Flathead V-8 and it came as a response to the growing influence of General Motors and the need for more power. It debuted in 1932 as part of Ford's effort to give its cars and trucks power, but it came to define the company for many years to come.

There had been V-8 engines in vehicles before, but they were mostly too expensive for the average person.

This 1954 F-100 has a Power King V-8 engine under its hood.

23

By including the V-8 in a light truck, Henry Ford made the powerful motor available to just about anybody. Instead of providing power through six cylinders, the Flathead used eight. That meant two more pistons pumping inside the truck's core and more power when drivers hit the gas.

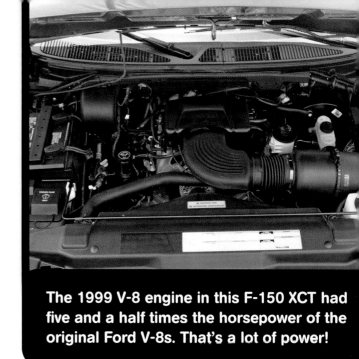

The 1999 V-8 engine in this F-150 XCT had five and a half times the horsepower of the original Ford V-8s. That's a lot of power!

Sure, there were some problems at first. But they were corrected quickly. By 1933 Ford was offering customers the opportunity to enjoy the V-8 in pickups.

There was still the opportunity to get a four-cylinder engine in a Ford, but the V-8 was new and it was popular. With only 65 **horsepower,** it didn't give drivers race-car strength, but Ford sales went up anyway.

The Flathead ruled the Ford truck world until 1954, when it was retired.

During the 1970s most Ford pickups sported a V-6 engine, like this 1974 version, which helped save on gas.

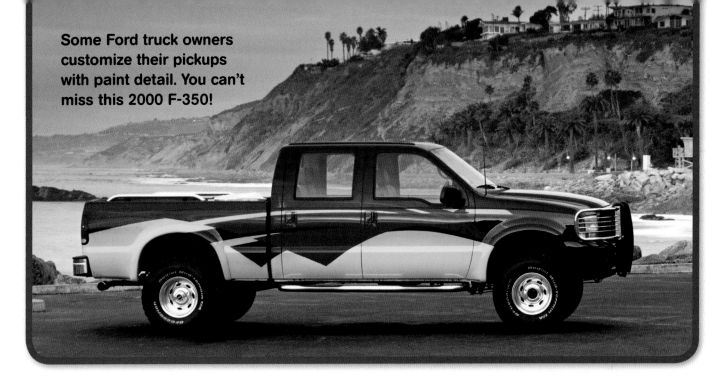
Some Ford truck owners customize their pickups with paint detail. You can't miss this 2000 F-350!

The replacement was another V-8 called the Power King. And oh, how things changed in just twenty-two years. The King generated 130 horsepower, twice what the Flathead had produced, even though it was the same size.

Ford moved through the 1950s and 1960s mixing power with economy. Although the emphasis placed on miles-per-gallon ratings was much less than in today's world, Ford was still interested in saving its drivers money on fuel. In 1960 the V-8 received some upgrades that improved gas mileage. In 1962, Ford went so far as to advertise its economy: "Save on gas . . . save on oil . . . save on tires . . . every day you drive!" That's how Ford put it, and America responded.

Harley motorcycle or Ford pickup? Why choose when you can have this special edition 2004 Harley-Davidson Super Duty! It combines the comfort of a truck with the cool sound of a bike.

As the 1960s rolled into the 1970s, Ford not only kept the V-8 as a standard, it also offered more powerful engines. Some produced nearly 150 horsepower. But the base models of Ford pickups were soon sporting V-6 engines that were plenty powerful but offered more reasonable gas mileage. It was still possible to get a V-8, but it often required diesel fuel, or it came only in Ford's biggest, most heavy-duty pickups, like the F-350.

Ford continued to blend power and value in its trucks as it headed into the twenty-first century, but it still had some tricks to pull. In 1999 the F-150 Lightning model had a supercharged V-8 that generated 360 horsepower. In 2000 Ford teamed with Harley-Davidson, America's most famous motorcycle maker, to create the Harley-Davidson F-150. Not only was it a cool-looking truck; it also had an exhaust system that produced the same **rumble** Harley bikes made. And for those with a real need for speed, there was the SVT Lightning, the world's fastest truck. It reached 140 miles per hour (225 kilometers per hour) and could get there pretty quickly.

It was yet another Ford innovation, something America had come to expect of its top truck maker.

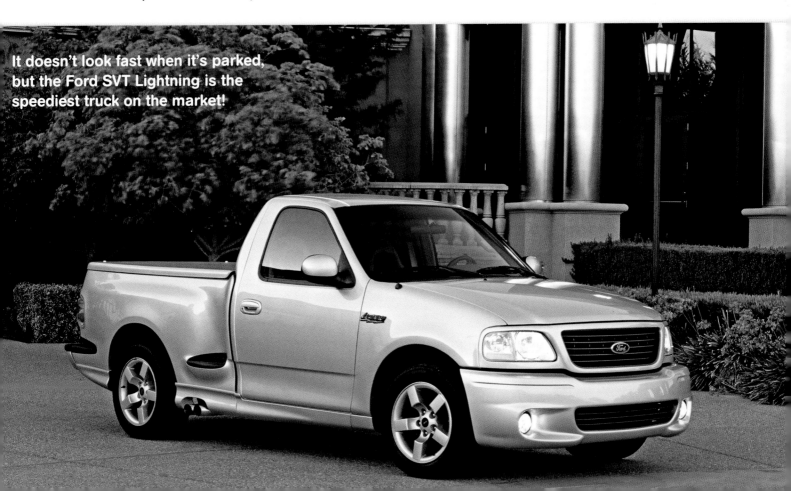

It doesn't look fast when it's parked, but the Ford SVT Lightning is the speediest truck on the market!

Vital Statistics

1948 Ford F-1 Pickup

Power: 275 hp
Engine Size: 351 ci/5.75L
Engine Type: V-8
Weight: 3,120 lbs (1,415 kg)
Top Speed: 105 mph (169 km/h)

2008 Ford F-450 Super Duty Pickup

Power: **350 hp**
Engine Size: **390 ci/6.4 L**
Engine Type: **PowerStroke turbo diesel V-8**
Weight: **9,360 lbs (4,246 kg)**
Top Speed: **100 mph (161 km/h)**
0–60 mph (0–96.5 km/h): **8.9 sec**

GLOSSARY

budget	The amount a person can afford to spend.
chassis	The frame and wheels of a motor vehicle, but not the engine or body.
crisis	A time of tremendous danger or trouble.
debut	The first time something appears in public.
decal	A picture or design that can be stuck onto various things, including a car or truck.
eight-cylinder engine	An engine that has eight pistons moving up and down.
famine	A time in which there is not enough food for people, leading to great hardship and often death for many.
forefront	The place where things happen first.
framework	A structure that serves as the base for something that will be built upon it.
Great Depression	The ten years of great poverty in America caused by the stock market crash of 1929.
hauler	A truck that can carry or pull something heavy.
horsepower	A way to measure the power of an engine. The greater the horsepower (hp), the stronger the engine.
momentum	The force created by the onrush of events.
outfit	To equip something to make it operate more successfully.
requirement	A need in a certain situation.
rumble	A deep, heavy sound, like thunder.
severe	Harsh or especially tough.
spiralounge seat	A driver's-side seat in a truck with a spring that adjusts to the driver's weight and a shock absorber for a smoother ride.
transmission	The part of an engine that allows it to change gears and move faster.

FURTHER INFORMATION

BOOKS

Henshaw, Peter. *The Ultimate Encyclopedia of Pickups*. Edison, NJ: Chartwell Books, Inc., 2007.

McLaughlin, Paul G. *Ford Medium-Duty Trucks*. Hudson, WI: Iconografix, 2006.

WEB SITES

www.fordf150.net

www.ford-trucks.com

www.fordvehicles.com/truck

About the Author

MICHAEL BRADLEY is a writer and broadcaster who lives near Philadelphia. He has written for *Sports Illustrated for Kids*, *Hoop*, *Inside Stuff*, and *Slam* magazines and is a regular contributor to Comcast SportsNet in Philadelphia.

INDEX

Page numbers in **boldface** are photographs.